# *The Prestige*

# Nottingha

## John Banks

### Additional information from F P Groves

# All Photographs by G H F Atkins

**© 2002 J M Banks & G H F Atkins**

**ISBN 1 898432 18 X**

*Front cover:* The last standard Nottingham trolleybus was the BUT six-wheeler. Number **507** (**KTV 507**), front wheel chocked against the slight gradient, awaits its departure time. The picture was taken in January 1964.

*Back cover:* In the period covered by this book Nottingham's standard bus design changed from traditional front-engined buses to those with engines at the back and the entrance at the front under the control of the driver.

*Title page:* Number **213** (**UTV 213**) was one of the first 30 AEC Regent Mark V buses new to Nottingham in 1955/6. They had Park Royal bodywork, 9.6-litre engines and manual gearboxes.

*Below:* Parliament Street garage has been the principal depot for the Nottingham fleet since the late nineteen-twenties, when it was known as Carter Gate. In its early years it housed trams, trolleybuses and motor-buses. By the time of this March 1972 view the trams and trolleybuses were long gone and the garage was host to Daimler Fleetlines and Leyland Atlanteans with Metro-Cammell bodywork to Nottingham specification.

*>> Opposite page:* Milton Street, Nottingham, outside Victoria station, on 1st July 1966. The previous day had witnessed the last trolleybus operation in the city. Number **506** (**KTV 506**), a 1950 BUT, was being used on a special last trolleybus journey.

*Prewar and wartime scenes...* The west end of the Old Market Square in about 1937 (above) was host to two of the 1935 Metro-Cammell-bodied Leyland trolleybuses on the Trent Bridge - Bulwell service. The private cars are equally redolent of the era: a 1937 Vauxhall 14 with characteristic box boot was in the foreground and a Morris or Wolseley (they were almost identical - an early example of badge-engineering) was turning right in front of Griffin & Spalding's department store. The cars parked at the kerb, the lady leaving the red telephone kiosk with its "A" and "B" buttons, the lack of yellow lines and festoons of restrictive signs and the absence of litter are further reminders of a more gentle age in which, despite the hardness of the times, municipal pride figured strongly. The 1939-45 war, which was to become known as the Second World War, was round the corner, however, and the people of Nottingham, as everywhere else in the country and much of the rest of the world, were about to be severely tested. In the picture below, taken at the Wells Road (Kildare Road) terminus during the war, No. **338** (**TV 4476**), one of the 1931 Brush-bodied Ransomes trolleybuses, shows the white-painted additions to its livery for use during blackout conditions. No gas masks are being carried by the pedestrians, suggesting that this picture was taken towards the end of the war.

*A sign of the times...*

*In about 1950, opposite Elmswood Gardens, where the photographer then had his home, the tram tracks along the main road, in disuse since before the war, were being lifted by a gang using a Nottingham Corporation Dennis lorry.*

## INTRODUCTION

At the outbreak of War in September 1939, Nottingham City Transport had a motor bus fleet composed entirely of AECs: there were 216 double-deck Regents of which 38 had petrol engines and 9 single-deckers of which four were 1929 AEC Reliances with petrol engines and the other five were modern 1937 oil-engined Regals. There were also 125 trolleybuses dating from between 1930 and 1935. On 30th September 1939, three of the remaining AEC Reliances were withdrawn and sold for ARP use and on 1st November 1939, 27 of the 1931 petrol-engined Regents were delicenced due to fuel rationing and the reduction of services. This all took place with a new General Manager , Ben England, in charge; he had started his duties on 17th September 1939, following the early death of J L Gunn in April 1939.

Action was taken urgently to black out the vehicles and all windows were blue-lacquered and interior lights screened to prevent light getting out to the rear platform. After about a month, the 1938/9 motorbuses had blinds fitted to the front windows and to two windows on each side of both decks and the lacquer removed. Some of the trolleybuses with traction voltage lighting were fitted with blinds on all

windows and the lacquer was removed from these too.

In June 1940, after the evacuation of the British Expeditionary Force from Dunkerque when invasion was believed to be imminent, "Nottingham" was removed from the sides of all vehicles and for a time in June and July all destination indicators were blank. In order to reduce flashing caused by the trolley wheels, these were replaced by carbon slides which also reduced wear on the overhead equipment. Some of the petrol-engined Regents delicensed in November 1939 were brought back into service in late 1940 and early 1941.

In 1939, a programme of converting AEC A171 7.7 litre indirect injection engines to type A173 direct injection had begun following delivery of the 45 1937 Regents, ten of which had the then new A173 engines, as did all 46 examples of the 1938-9 Regents when new. This programme was continued during the war and extended to the 8.8 litre A165 engines which became type A180 being completed in the year ended 31st March 1947, after which no indirect injection engines remained in the fleet.

A shortage of trolleybuses was felt when service 46 (Trent Bridge - Old Market Square) was reintroduced to replace motor buses on services which crossed the City Centre to reach Trent Bridge; there were also further peak

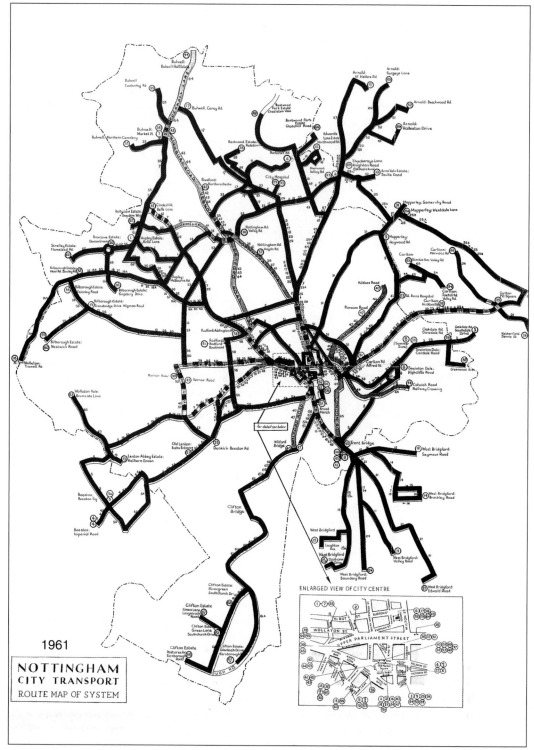

**1961**

**NOTTINGHAM CITY TRANSPORT**
ROUTE MAP OF SYSTEM

ENLARGED VIEW OF CITY CENTRE

*(John C Gillham Collection/Nottingham City Transport)*

period commitments for trolleybuses elsewhere in the city.

In October 1940 four 1937/8 Park Royal-bodied AEC 661T two-axle trolleybuses were acquired from Cleethorpes and put to work on the Nottingham Road route. Two much older trolleybuses were also acquired in 1940, from Southend on Sea. These were English Electric vehicles dating from 1930; numbered 302-3 in the Nottingham fleet, they were intended mainly for use at peak periods.

Further second-hand trolleybuses were acquired in 1941, one being a Weymann-bodied Daimler CTM4 demonstrator, new in 1938. This was licensed in February, numbered 441 and joined the ex-Cleethorpes AECs on the Nottingham Road route. Later in 1941, six Guy BTX single-deck trolleybuses with Ransomes 32-seat centre-entrance bodies dating from 1928/9 arrived from Hastings and were numbered 304-9. At first these were used on the Trent Bridge to Wollaton Park via Derby Road route but were later reallocated for use as peak period extras on other services based at Parliament Street.

Nottingham suffered a severe air raid on the night of 8th/9th May 1941 and damage, which cost £5,900 to rectify, was caused to the Parliament Street Depot and Head Office. Although no direct hit was made there were several near misses with some buildings nearby being destroyed and windows were broken on 103 motorbuses and ten trolleybuses; two of the motorbuses, 256 and 258, were extensively damaged. There were disruptions to trolleybus services because of overhead wires being brought down and unexploded bombs closed certain roads.

The remaining petrol-engined buses were brought out of store in 1941 to meet increasing demands and two Regents, 124/5, which had been hired to Coventry Corporation in April 1941, returned in September and were placed in service. The Reliance towing vehicle was

**Return of the AEC Regent**
*Typifying the early 1950s and the re-emergence of the AEC Regent in the Nottingham fleet, No. **340** (**KTV 340**) was one of 71 Regent IIIs delivered in 1949/50. It had a Roberts 56-seat body. These were NCT's first 8ft-wide motorbuses.*

converted back to a motorbus and two other Reliances, 77 and 81, were returned from police service in December 1941 and had the seating converted to perimeter-type to provide standing room for 30 passengers. Three ADC single-deck buses built in 1928/9 were acquired from West Bridgford UDC and these buses, which were the oldest in the fleet, were numbered 69-71. At first they ran in West Bridgford's maroon and cream livery with Nottingham transfers but later assumed normal NCT livery.

During 1941 the Ministry of War Transport had advised Nottingham that a number of trolleybus chassis destined for Johannesburg had become available for UK operators and the General Manager was authorised to ask for eight. Initially ten were allocated to Nottingham but this was later reduced to five and they were to be bodied by Weymann to wartime specification. These vehicles, which were Sunbeam MF2 two-axled chassis were not delivered until September 1942, and took the numbers 447-51. They were the first eight-feet wide vehicles in the fleet and were allocated to the Carlton - Wollaton Park service. Because the

Johannesburg trolleybuses had regenerative control equipment with their compound-wound 103 hp motors, some modifications had to be made to the power distribution system by the fitting of sectionalising switches linking mercury-arc fed sections with those fed by rotary converters, thus spreading any overloads. The ex-Hastings vehicles also had regenerative control equipment.

Production of motorbuses and trolleybuses to wartime specifications commenced during 1942. Orders for these vehicles were placed by the Ministry of Supply (MOS) and allocations to operators were made by the Ministry of War Transport (MOWT). Nottingham received 31 trolleybuses and 43 motorbuses under these arrangements from 1942 to 1946 (trolleybuses) and 1943 to 1945 (motorbuses). The trolleybuses had Karrier W chassis and bodies by Weymann, Park Royal, Brush or Roe, and apart from 452-8 of 1944 with English Electric 408C 115 hp motors with regenerative control, all had BTH 207 85 hp motors. The motorbuses comprised 17 Guy Arabs with Gardner 5LW engines and bodywork by Massey, Pickering or Weymann, and 26 Daimler CWA6s with AEC A173 7.7 litre engines and bodies by Northern Counties, Brush or Duple. Guy No. 87 of 1944 had an experimental bearerless metal-framed Weymann body, one of a small number tried out by various operators. Nottingham's wartime vehicles were withdrawn between 1956 and 1963.

It proved impossible to obtain any new vehicles before 1948, and it was decided to have the bodywork of the Cravens bodied Regents of 1937 completely reconditioned. Cravens themselves undertook the rebuilding of the first examples in 1946 but later the work was transferred to other coachbuilders. The rebuilding work contined until later in 1948, and the opportunity was taken to increase the seating capacity of these buses from 52 to 54, as originally specified, due to an increase in their maximum permitted unladen weight. The seating increase was not applied to the few Cravens bodies which were rebuilt in the Trent Bridge works. The three Cravens single-deckers were also reconditioned in Trent Bridge Works, the wartime longitudinal seating being replaced by prewar coach-type seats. Some second-hand motorbuses were acquired during 1947: first

were four 1937/8 Thornycroft double-deckers with Park Royal bodies from Southampton, who had fitted wartime type wooden seats in place of the upholstered originals before the transfer. They became Nottingham numbers 122-5.

Later in 1947, two petrol-engined 1930 AEC Regent motorbuses which had Ransomes 49-seat highbridge bodywork similar to the London ST type were acquired from West Bridgford and were numbered 118/9 in the Nottingham fleet. Four 1937 Regents with 8.8 litre oil engines and Park Royal 56-seat bodies were acquired from Halifax and were numbered 259-62 and before the end of 1947, two more petrol-engined 1931 AEC Regents were obtained from West Bridgford; these had Brush 52-seat bodies and were numbered 116/7.

Permission had been granted in February 1946 for the operation of 8ft wide vehicles on certain roads enabling NCT to run 30 trolleybuses of that width on service 39 between Carlton and Wollaton Park and 41 motorbuses on the Sherwood and Arnold routes.

Ten Daimler CVD6 chassis with Brush bodies were ordered during 1947 and were expected in September that year but they were not delivered until July/August 1948, numbered 270-9. A British Exhibition took place in Copenhagen during September 1948, and at the request of Daimler, one of this batch, 278, was one of six Daimlers sent to the Danish capital to convey the general public from 1st September until 9th October. In the meantime, eleven 1934 Karrier and Ransomes trolleybuses had their bodywork rebuilt by outside contractors from 1948 until early 1949.

It had been stated in 1947 when the four ex-Halifax motorbuses were acquired that eight vehicles would be available, but later the Halifax Transport Committee decided to dispose of their surplus buses by auction. The Nottingham General Manager was therefore authorised to attend the auction in 1948 to buy a number of these buses and seven were puchased at a total cost of £4,220. These seven comprised one petrol-engined and six oil-engined AEC Regents dating from 1934 to 1937. Four had their bodies reconditioned by Nudd Bros & Lockyer before entering service between May and July. One of them, JX 1790, had been the first bus to be sent to London in October 1940 because of damage to the LPTB fleet in the blitz. Of the seven buses from Halifax which took Nottingham numbers 263-9, five had Park Royal and two had Roberts bodywork and two, Nottingham 263/4, were from the same 1937 batch as the four obtained in 1947.

Four Karrier W and 13 BUT 9611T trolleybus chassis, all two-axle, had been due to be fitted with Metro-Cammell bodies in 1947 but it was stated by Met-Camm that they could not be delivered until the end of 1948. The order was transferred to Charles H Roe, of Leeds, and the four Karriers were delivered in July 1948 with fleet numbers 479-82, whilst the 13 BUTs came in October as 483-95. The Karriers and BUT No. 493 had automatic acceleration.

As was the case for so many other operators in the 1947-9 period, deliveries of new post-war buses improved in 1949. Roberts-bodied Daimlers 280-94 arrived first; before all these had been delivered, 30 Metro-Cammell-bodied AEC Regents, 97-126, started to appear.

Later in the year, the first 16 of the 41 AEC Regents with Roberts bodies, 301-41, the first 8ft-wide motorbuses in the fleet, arrived and with the delivery of a further six Brush bodied Daimler CVD6s, 295-300, in the summer, 66 new motorbuses had been taken into stock, enabling the withdrawal of a large number of petrol- and early oil-engined buses. The first two BUT 9641T three-axled 8ft-wide trolleybuses were placed in service in December 1949. Numbered 500/1, they were the first new six-wheelers since 1935 and as 70-seaters they had the largest seating capacity of any vehicles in the NCT fleet.

There was a changeover from ticket punches and ticket machines to Bell Punch Ultimate equipment in 1949, which was largely completed by the end of the year and this led to great savings in clerical work and time.

The remainder of the Roberts-bodied AEC Regents were delivered during the early part of 1950 and these resulted in the withdrawal of the last petrol-engined double-deckers and the last AEC Reliance. The remaining three-axled 8ft-wide trolleybuses, 502-24, were delivered by May 1950. Seventeen of the Brush bodied 7ft 6ins-wide BUT three-axled type also arrived in 1950; they were sent to Bulwell Depot to work on service 44.

1951 and 1952 saw the delivery of the rest of the BUT three-axled trolleybuses, and the fleet number series from 500 to 601 was complete; these were to be Nottingham's last new trolleybuses. The additional vehicles were allocated to Bulwell and Trent Bridge depots. Apart from four AEC Regal Mark III single-deckers with East Lancashire Coachbuilders 35-seat bodies, numbers 701-4, delivered in June 1951, there were no new motorbuses in 1951 and 1952, but in order to serve the Clifton Estate to the south of the River Trent, over which there had been protracted public sittings of the Traffic Commissioners with West Bridgford UDC, Barton Transport Ltd and the South Notts Bus Co. Ltd all involved, NCT commenced running into the estate from late October 1952. The initial route was via Wilford Lane and this was crossed near Wilford Village by a low bridge of the former Great Central Railway, which provided only limited headroom. Lowbridge double-deck buses were necessary and seven 1945 Daimler CWA6 double-deckers with Duple 55-seat bodies to wartime design were obtained second-hand from Bradford City Transport and given Nottingham fleet numbers 44-50. Two were prepared for the start of the new service, the other five appearing during the ensuing 14 months.

Other housing developments in the city were also being served by new facilities, mostly by the extension of existing services. Some curtailments also took place in 1952, including Nottingham's first trolleybus abandonment when in March, the 36 and 48 services were cut back by about 200 yards to terminate at the junction of Nottingham Road and Valley Road instead of running through to Vernon Road. The overhead linking Nottingham Road with Vernon Road was dismantled.

January 1953 saw the opening of a new bus garage at Bilborough to take the pressure off the overcrowded main garage at Lower Parliament Street. The Notts and Derby trolleybus route between Nottingham and Ripley was abandoned on 25th April and the next day saw a complete reorganisation of the trolleybus services along Nottingham Road with a new service, numbered 41, between Cinderhill crossroads and Trent Bridge over the former Notts and Derby route and an augmented service 36 between Valley Road and the city centre at King Street. Three demonstration vehicles were used in the city during 1953 and early 1954: a 60-passenger

(36 seated) Duple-bodied Daimler underfloor-engined motorbus with a rear entrance and front exit; a single-deck BUT trolleybus for Glasgow having an East Lancs body, with rear entrance and centre exit, with 27 seats and provision for 27 standing passengers; and, in January 1954, a prototype AEC Regent double-decker with Park Royal bodywork of medium weight construction and a syncromesh gearbox.

In June 1953 delivery began of the first of an order for 112 8ft-wide AEC Regent Mark III motorbuses with preselective gearboxes and Park Royal 56-seat bodies, numbered 127 upwards. Ordered in 1948, these were delayed pending the completion of Bilborough garage. The intial batch comprised Nos 127-67 in June 1953 to March 1954. Then followed ten lowbridge Park Royal 53-seat examples, 199-208, delivered between April and June 1954. From July to October 1954, 31 more highbridge buses, 168-98, to the same specification as 127-67 arrived; following the latest fashion these had directional flashing indicators instead of semaphore arms. Even with 127-208 delivered and in service, there still remained 30 Regents outstanding from the 112 originally ordered. These were delivered as Regent Mark Vs with syncromesh gearboxes and the lighter type of Park Royal body, seating 61, which had recently been introduced. They had exposed radiators and the body was of four-bay construction rather than the five-bay design favoured previously. These 30 were numbered 209-38 and arrived between September 1955 and March 1956. Like the Mark III Regents before them they had 9.6 litre engines.

Thirty-five further Mark V Regents, 239-73, similar to 209-38 but with 62 seats, were delivered between September and November 1956.

When tenders for the next batch of 44 buses, to replace most of the remaining prewar and wartime buses were sought in 1957, Leyland Motors Ltd submitted the lowest and the choice for bodywork was the Metro-Cammell Orion but of a special design with only four bays per side, Nos 2-33 being steel-framed and 34-45 alloy-framed. The steel-framed examples were over half a ton heavier than the alloy-framed vehicles. Numbers 2-33 arrived between February and April 1958 and 34-45 in January and February 1959. They were Nottingham's first Leyland motorbuses and almost spelt the end for the traditional AECs which had been the major presence in the Nottingham fleet since 1930.

The trolleybus fleet, which had been maintained at 155 vehicles from 1953 to 1959, was reduced by 15 in 1960 and some peak period trolleybus workings were taken over by motorbuses.

A change in livery style was made in 1961 to green lower saloons and cream upper saloons with green bands round the cantrail and with green roofs. The earlier examples had cream upper deck window pillars, changed to green on later buses.

No new buses were taken into the fleet for more than three years until October 1962 and by then it had been decided to abandon the trolleybus system in stages. Eighteen of the newly introduced Daimler Fleetline double-decker with front entrance and a transverse rear-mounted Gardner 6LX engine were delivered between October and December 1962, numbered 46-63. They had Park Royal 77-seat bodywork and were 30ft long and 8ft wide. Number 63 of this series was repainted experimentally in a predominantly green livery in 1963, but the experiment was not continued.

The first trolleybus service to be converted from trolleybus to motorbus operation was service 45 between Wollaton Park and Trent Bridge in November 1962. No further changeovers took place until the mid-1960s when five stages of trolleybus abandonment took place between April and October 1965 with a final stage, the Nottingham Road route, on 1st July 1966.

There was a change of General Manager late in 1962 when Ben England retired and John C Wake from Bradford was appointed.

In the meantime, the second batch of rear-engined double-deckers arrived between June and December 1963. These were numbered 64-94 and were further Daimler Fleetlines with Gardner 6LX engines but with Northern Counties bodywork, again 30ft by 8ft and seating 77. Specifications were discussed in 1962 with Northern Counties and it was natural to insist on interchangeable windows, seats, cushions, lighting fixtures, panels and other features. These buses had many weight saving features and weighed 3cwts less than the 1962

Park Royal batch. When specifications were being considered for 126 buses which would be required in 1964/5, mainly for trolleybus replacement, tenders were accepted for 42 traditional half-cab AEC Renowns with MCW or Northern Counties bodies, and for 84 Leyland PDR1/2 Atlanteans with Northern Counties or MCW bodies. Standardisation was the aim and all 126 buses had 6ft 1in headroom in the lower saloon and 6ft in the upper saloon with interchangeable windows, seats, door-equipment and many other fittings; the Atlantean chassis had the Daimler Fleetline gearbox with transfer box. In 1964, with use of the BET windscreen, an obvious visual style, peculiar to Nottingham and to become known as the "Nottingham Look", began.

More AEC Renowns, Daimler Fleetlines and Leyland Atlanteans were bought and in September 1968 neighbouring West Bridgford Urban District Council's bus fleet was taken over by NCT and the 28 vehicles transferred from the Abbey Road premises in West Bridgford to Lower Parliament Street garage. Thus, NCT inherited more AECs, including some Regent Mk III double-deckers some of which dated from 1947.

Another 1968 milestone was the New Bus Grant system under which vehicles constructed to a Government-approved specification and first licensed after 1st September attracted a grant of 25% of the purchase price. Nottingham's first Grant vehicles were 22 Leyland Atlantean double-deckers and six AEC Swifts, all with Northern Counties bodies. The Atlantean double deckers had certain features not found on any other buses in the fleet. The Grant was increased to 50% of the purchase price in late 1971.

Rear-engined, front-entrance double-deckers were now the standard, but in April/May 1972, two Bedford YRQ coaches to Bus Grant specification were taken into the fleet. They had Willowbrook Expressway 45-seat bodies and were intended to operate private hires and also journeys on lighter loaded services.

In 1972, the City Council adopted its new Transportation Policy. This was intended to reduce the number of motor cars entering the city centre area at the peak periods by improving public transport facilties. Bus services on main radial routes were to be increased by about one third, a new free city centre bus service was to be introduced and, as an experiment, a Zone and Collar scheme was to be introduced on main roads in the west of the city to make it difficult for cars to enter the city centre. As it was intended to run one-man-operated buses on the increased services, it was necessary to buy new vehicles as no operators were then disposing of omo buses. Eighty-seven extra buses would be required for the increased peak frequencies, at least eight single deckers for the free city centre service and 18 coaches would be required for the park & ride services from the special car parks being set up in the Zone & Collar area.

The first of the new services to commence, in November 1972, was the initial city centre service, 88. Four new Leyland National two-door 46 seaters were hired from London Country Bus Services (they were delivered direct to Nottingham from the Leyland factory at Workington). Their roofs were painted orange with the legend CENTRAL AREA SERVICES in black lettering on the cove panels. The service commenced in November 1972 and was extremely successful. In the same month a Saturday Park & Ride service was introduced from the Forest, an area of open land about one mile north of the City Centre where the annual Goose Fair takes place each October. This was (and still is) a commercially operated service using double-deck buses; the charge in 1972 was 10 pence per car and is now (in 2002) £1.50.

In 1973 peak period frequencies were augmented; to cope with this, older double deckers which were due to be replaced by new Daimler Fleetlines were retained. The fleet-strength thus began to increase and between March and June the first peak period increases were implemented. Further increases were implemented in October 1973 and then at regular intervals until 1976.

In January 1973, it was decided to introduce a second Central Area Service, on a mainly east/west axis to complement the existing service 88 which was arranged on a mainly north/south axis in an anti-clockwise direction, as soon as the necessary vehicles could be obtained. It was estimated that to operate two services, eight buses would be required, nine on Wednesday, Friday and Saturday as service 88 had been strengthened to a four-minute headway because of increased loadings. For this, sixteen two-door Leyland Nationals were ordered. The Central Area services, being free, were not regarded as Stage Carriage and buses used entirely on these services would not qualify for New Bus Grant. If these buses could run more than 50% of their mileage on ordinary services, Bus Grant would be given, thus it was sometimes necessary to run 1969 AEC Swifts on service 88 when the London Country Nationals were in Nottingham, mainly on Wednesday, Friday and Saturday, and two of these had orange roofs and CENTRAL AREA SERVICE in black letters. The four London Country Nationals were returned in July/August 1973 and service 77, the second Central Area service, commenced on 30th July.

In November 1973, the General Manager, John Wake, retired and was succeeded by F P Groves, who had been Deputy General Manager since June 1972

In 1974, the 18 coaches required for the Zone and Collar Park & Ride services were ordered; Leyland PSU3/4RB Leopard chassis and Duple Dominant coach bodies to Bus Grant specification were called for. They were lilac with waistbands in Mercedes Red, and became known as "Lilac Leopards". When the Zone & Collar services ceased in 1976, 14 (Nos 13-25/8) of the "Lilac Leopards" were sold to Maidstone Borough Transport.

The Park & Ride services for which the 18 coaches had been obtained commenced in July 1975 but the loadings were disappointing and drivers still found ways round the Zone and Collar and continued to use their cars. Following a change in political control of Nottingham City Council in May 1976, the Park and Ride services were withdrawn in the July and the Council also required City Transport to eliminate the deficit on its services by May 1979; a consequence of this was that the recently increased peak period frequencies had to be reduced again.

One of the problems of the 1970s was the late delivery of new buses which had been ordered for phased delivery so that there would be an intake of about 25-30 new buses each year in Nottingham's case. Thus 25 Fleetlines with Willowbrook bodies should have been delivered in 1974 and 25 more with Northern Counties

bodies in each of the years 1975 and 1976. There was a hold-up of new Fleetline chassis through Leyland, who had taken over Daimler in the 1960s, moving Fleetline production from Coventry to Leyland. Furthermore, because of production problems at Leyland, only about nine chassis were being produced each week rather than the 28 which had been built at Coventry. In the event, the 25 Fleetlines which should have been built with Willowbrook bodies lost their "slot" in Willowbrook's production arrangements and had to be sub-contracted to Northern Counties who built the first ten early in 1976 and the second 15 between August and November that year.

In spring 1975, one of the coach body dealers, Kirkby, advised NCT that up to 10 Leopards with Duple Dominant coach bodies were under construction and it was agreed that these should be obtained but finished as buses rather than coaches. Thus they had coach shells with 53 bus seats and a space for parcels and shopping at the front nearside. They were painted cream with green waistbands and had windows with sliding ventilators. They were known as "White Leopards" unofficially just as the 18 coaches of 1974/5 had become known as "Lilac Leopards". They proved useful vehicles, helping to plug the shortage of new buses and enabled the withdrawal of some older buses to take place. Fourteen more Duple-bodied Leopards were later obtained as well as one bodied by Willowbrook

Older Fleetlines 75/7 and 82/3 were sent to Northern Counties late in 1975 for rebodying. Completed by April 1976, the new single-door bodies were to the Nottingham specification but lacked a rear engine bulkhead. The lower-deck rear seats were backed by a full width rear window in much the same way as Volvo Citybuses of 1980 onwards. One other chassis was rebodied, the former 466, which had been damaged by fire in 1974. The chassis had been rebuilt and East Lancashire fitted a new two-door body, and the bus reappeared in April 1976 as fleet number 500.

Forty-five Fleetlines of the order for 60 due for delivery in 1975 and 1976 were still outstanding in 1977 and the chassis order was changed to specify AN68 Atlanteans in view of the successful operation of that type. Among the Atlanteans of that period was No. 666, displayed at the Motor Show in November 1978, which had a striking new style of body though based on the standard Nottingham structure. It had single windscreens with bonded windows and the front entrance was of single width.

Many more AN68s were bought, but when the model was phased out by Leyland, thoughts turned to new double-deckers for the future and two each of the new Dennis Falcon V, Leyland Olympian and Volvo Citybus models were assessed. The Olympians were heavy, at 10,160 kg, compared with 9,900 kg for the Falcons and 9,378 kg for the Citybuses. The first Falcon, 396, was exhibited at the NEC Motor Show in October 1982.

F P Groves retired as General Manager in February 1983 and was succeeded by D Deakin who continued as General Manager until October 1986 and then became Managing Director of Nottingham City Transport Limited on Deregulation.

The move towards smaller buses, often little more than converted delivery vans, gained momentum in Nottingham in the 1980s and the coach fleet was also strengthened during the 1980s and 1990s and now totals 13. The bus fleet took in 14 Volvo Citybuses and 12 Mark II Leyland National 52-seaters in 1985. At Deregulation in October 1986, NCT retained almost all its network though some journeys were withdrawn on certain services at first.

In November 1988, NCT took over Erewash Valley Services Ltd, based in Ilkeston, which had been owned previously by Stevensons. This was a short-lived venture and NCT soon relinquished its interest, though some NCT vehicles were transferred to Erewash Valley including some of the "White Leopards". The business of the Gotham-based independent

South Notts Bus Co Ltd was purchased in 1991 and a further acquisition has been that of Pathfinder, of Newark, running services between Newark and Nottingham. NCT first acquired the share capital and then merged it into the main operation in November 1998. In the decade or so up to and into the new millennium the fleet has retained its position as one of the most distinctive and modern in the country. Among the latest double-deckers are some designed to carry up to 99 passengers and trams are scheduled to reappear in the city in November 2003.

The undertaking now has a French partner and will certainly maintain its position as one of the most interesting and characteristic operators in the country.

Once again Philip Groves has been of inestimable help with his work on the Introduction and captions. Roy Marshall has read the text and suggested several improvements and David and Mary Shaw have read the proofs for all those annoying little typographicals that a writer never spots in his own work. Grateful thanks to all.

Every photograph in the book was taken by Geoffrey Atkins, the earliest in 1929, the latest in 2001: a span of 72 years in nine decades - surely a record. The book and its companion, Volume One published in January 2002, are jointly intended as a tribute to Geoffrey Atkins on his 90th birthday. Author and publisher must once again go on record with their thanks to Geoffrey for so courteously and willingly making his life's work available for these and other books in *The Prestige Series*.

*John Banks*
*Romiley, Cheshire*
*February 2002*

*Nottingham demonstrators*

There had been in Nottingham - and would be again in the postwar years - frequent use of demonstrators from the various manufacturers. All municipalities, and other operators, were the legitimate targets of the manufacturers' salesmen and the ability to offer a bus on loan for even a week, and often for longer, was a powerful tool in the salesman's armoury. Two of the most interesting demonstrators to run in the city had been a Thornycroft BC, **OU 4028**, with Strachan bodywork, seen *(above)* in Angel Row on 8th March 1930 and London Transport's **RT19 (FXT 194)**, in a green livery, photographed *(below)* at Mapperley in 1941. Neither Thornycrofts nor RTs were subsequently purchased new, although four 1936/7 Thornycroft Daring 56-seat Park Royal-bodied double-deckers were bought second-hand from Southampton Corporation in January 1947, and AEC Regents to the provincial pattern were bought in quantity as long as that model remained available.

*The AEC "Q"*

The prewar side-engined AEC "Q" double-decker did not sell well, despite its advanced specification, and of the few built none entered the Nottingham municipal fleet. One did, however, run in the city for a short time as a demonstrator on service 11. As is so often the case with these fleeting demonstration visits, the Geoffrey Atkins collection contains the only known photographic record.

*Nottingham by night*

The quiet scene above, of AEC Regent **123** (**KTV 123**) in Long Row in September 1949, contrasts with the bustle of the lower picture, in which a Daimler passes beneath trolleybus wires glistening in the reflected light and an AEC Regent in the background heels over alarmingly as it negotitates the one-way system. Geoffrey Atkins's night scenes are one of the many strengths of his collection.

**_Traffic and hazards_**

**_Above:_** The Old Market Square in June 1953. The six buses and one trolleybus are the only visible motor vehicles in the summer sunlight. Despite the hardships still being felt in the fifties, that decade can in retrospect be seen to have been something of a golden age, lost forever. This picture epitomises the era.

**_Below:_** Metro-Cammell-bodied AEC Regent No. **120** (**KTV 120**) negotiating tarmac-laying operations at Gregory Boulevard on a dull April day in 1952.

### Second-hand trolleybuses

Nottingham was fortunate to be able to acquire five modern two-axle trolleybuses in 1940/1. Four AECs with Park Royal bodies came from Cleethorpes in October 1940, one (No. 437) dating from 1937 and the other three (Nos 438-40) built in 1938. In February 1941 a Daimler demonstrator with Weymann body to Hull Corporation specification was acquired. All five ran mainly on the Nottingham Road service. In the picture above, No. **440** (**AFU 155**) is shown in Milton Street, outside Victoria station, in August 1949; the Daimler, No. **441** (**GTO 741**), was at the King Street/Queen Street junction terminal point *(below)* in June of the same year.

***Wartime trolleybuses*** - The first new wartime trolleybuses in September and October 1942 comprised a batch of five Sunbeam MF2 8ft-wide vehicles with Weymann's 56-seat bodies built to an austere Ministry of Supply utility specification. The chassis had been diverted from an order for 25 placed by Johannesburg, South Africa. A dispensation had to be obtained to operate them, as 7ft 6ins was then the legal maximum width for a public service vehicle. For some years they were restricted to the Wollaton Park - City - Carlton service. Number **450** (**GTV 50**) was photographed *(above)* in Middleton Boulevard in July 1946. Number **443** (**GTV 43**) was a 1943 Karrier W with similar bodywork, seen *(below)* at Wilford Bridge in May 1949. It was one of a batch of four, Nos 442-5. The 1942 Sunbeams were Nos 447-51. There was never a fleet number 446. Both batches had upholstered seats from new.

### The King Street terminus

The terminal point in the city centre at the junction of King Street and Queen Street was a favourite spot for the photography of Nottingham and Notts & Derby trolleybuses. These pictures were taken there in May and August 1952. The upper view is of No. **445** (**GTV 45**), a 1944 Karrier W with Weymann's 56-seat bodywork, whilst the lower illustrates No. **454** (**GTV 654**), a similar chassis with bodywork by Park Royal. Not all Nottingham trolleybuses had battery-manoeuvring equipment, but No. 445 was one that did. These trolleybuses lasted in service until 1959 and 1962.

### Wartime bodywork variety

Nottingham's wartime utility trolleybuses managed to feature bodywork from a variety of manufacturers. This was frequently the case in those troubled times when all an operator could do was apply to the Ministry for new vehicles and be obliged to accept what was allocated. Ministry officials had little knowledge of the benefits of standardisation of units and were known to remind operators that they, the Ministry, decided what went where. Nottingham's No. **459** (**GTV 659**), a Roe-bodied Karrier W, was at the Hooton Road, Carlton, 38 terminus in September 1948. Number **468** (**GTV 668**) *(below)* was a similar chassis, bodied by Brush. It was photographed in January 1953. Both vehicles were 1945 deliveries; they were respectively withdrawn in 1963 and 1955.

## The "relaxed" utlity specification

The war over, a certain relaxation to the austere style of the Ministry-designed body was allowed: wooden slatted seats, for example, began to disappear and upholstered seats reappeared. Nottingham had ten Karrier W trolleybuses in 1946 with Park Royal 56-seat bodywork to this new style, of which No. **470** (**HAU 170**) is seen *(above)* in July 1946, when five months old, at Wollaton Park, Middleton Boulevard. In the scene below, at the junction of Mansfield Road and Middleton Boulevard in October 1951, No. **477** (**HAU 177**) of the same batch approaches the camera. Another utility trolleybus can be seen, as can a Mark I Standard Vanguard, a 1936/7 Morris and a prewar Hillman Minx. Traffic was quieter then: the cyclist appeared to be in no danger.

## Utility Guy Arabs

The Ministry specification also applied to wartime motorbuses. Unusually for an English operator, some of Nottingham's Mark I Guy Arabs, Nos 89-93 of April-June 1943, were bodied by Pickering, of Wishaw, Scotland. Number **92** (**GTV 412**) is shown *(above)*. It was at Manvers Street in September 1949. There were four more Guy Arabs in 1943, but these were Mark IIs with extended bonnets for the Gardner six-cylinder engine, which Nottingham never had, all their Guys having five-cylinder engines when new. This Massey-bodied quartet is represented by No. **96** (**GTV 416**), the last to be delivered, in September 1943. The photograph was taken at Parliament Street garage in June 1954. Both these Guy Arabs were withdrawn in 1956.

*Utility Guys and Daimlers*

*Above:* More Guy Arab Mark II buses came in 1944. Numbers 80-7 had Weymann's utility bodywork; one of them, No. **85** (**GTV 585**), was photographed on a works service in Granby Street in July 1956. The bus was withdrawn the following year. The last of the batch, No. 87, had an experimental bearerless metal-framed body and was later fitted with a Gardner 6LW engine. Note the loudspeaker on the lamp standard for relaying messages to intending passengers from the city centre inspector.

*Below:* Guy, Daimler, Bristol and Bedford built most of the United Kingdom's wartime buses. The first such Daimlers came to Nottingham in 1944. Nine CWA6 chassis with six-cylinder AEC engines managed to have bodywork from three different makers. Shown is No. **61** (**GTV 761**), one of four with Northern Counties bodies. Photographed at Trent Boulevard, West Bridgford, in August 1950, it was the first of Nottingham's utility Daimlers, delivered in May 1944, and was the last to be withdrawn, not going until 1959.

## Utility Daimlers

*Above:* Number **62** (**GTV 762**) of the Northern Counties-bodied 1944 quartet is shown in Stanhope Street, alongside Parliament Street garage, in March 1956, a year before its withdrawal. Utility bodies were modified in various ways as they became older, and in this case additional half-drop side-windows had been fitted, the destination screen rebuilt and upholstered seats fitted.

*Below:* The 1945 intake consisted of 17 Daimler CWA6 double-deckers, bodied by Duple Motor Bodies or Brush Coachworks, all as 56-seaters, ten of them to the relaxed austerity style. Duple-bodied No. **43** (**HAU 43**) was new to Nottingham in September 1945 and was photographed in Calverton Road, Arnold, in July 1949. This vehicle was fitted with upholstered seats, instead of the wooden slatted variety, from new. It served in Nottingham for eleven years and was withdrawn in 1956.

There was one basic Ministry of Supply design for the wartime and early postwar utility and relaxed utility bus bodies. Despite that, the various manufacturers managed to stamp their interpretations of the design with a certain individuality, making them, for the most part, readily recognisable one from another. In a pair of 1949 photographs taken at Parliament Street garage the similarities and differences between the Brush and Duple versions are shown. Number **69 (GTV 769)** *(above)*, a Brush example, was delivered into the fleet in November 1944, whereas No. **76 (GTV 876)**, with Duple body *(below)*, arrived in March 1945. They were 56-seaters and both were withdrawn in 1954. The use of bus panels for advertising was a mixed blessing. It brought revenue into an operator's coffers but was often visually unfortunate, although some observers used the advertisement to identify the vehicle from a distance. It was also fascinating to watch them being signwritten, a variety of bus advertising much to be preferred to the pasted paper versions seen elsewhere.

***Second-hand buses*** - The period of austerity that followed the ending of the war went on for longer than anyone could have foreseen. Food, fuel and clothing were rationed ("ration books" were as much a part of daily life as cheque books and credit cards are today) and raw materials for manufactured goods were in the direst short supply. Passenger numbers were increasing and new motor vehicles were hard to come by; most of those that were built were exported ("Export or Die" was the government of the day's slogan). Bus operators had to patch up their ageing prewar fleets and generally "make do and mend". The "making do" often involved buying second-hand buses from other operators. In 1947 Nottingham bought four petrol-engined AEC Regents from neighbouring West Bridgford: No. **119** (**VO 3878**) *(above)* was a 1930 Ransomes-bodied 49-seater built to the London General Omnibus Company's ST-type design; No. **117** (**VO 6819**) *(below)* dated from 1932 and was a Brush-bodied 52-seater. They lasted until 1949 and 1950.

### Second-hand buses

Further second-hand purchases in 1947 were of Thornycrofts from Southampton and AEC Regents from Halifax. Number **122** (**OW 9932**), a Thornycroft Daring DD5LW *(above)*, had been new in September 1936 as Southampton Corporation No. 6. The 56-seat body was by Park Royal. Three similar buses dating from 1937 became Nottingham's Nos 123-5. They were most unpopular with drivers and were quickly withdrawn, lasting only into 1948. Alongside is the last English Electric trolleybus to be withdrawn. Four 1937 AEC Regents acquired from the Halifax Joint Omnibus Committee, also in 1947, fitted into the Nottingham fleet rather better than had the Thornycrofts, and they were not withdrawn until 1954. Again with Park Royal 56-seat bodies, they are represented *(below)* by No. **261** (**JX 5270**).

## Second-hand buses

Further AEC Regents were bought from Halifax in 1948: five Park Royal 56-seaters and two 54-seaters with Roberts bodies. **JX 2304** *(above)* was one of the latter, which had been new in 1935; with the Nottingham fleet number **265** it had entered service, after reconditioning work by the coachbuilder Nudd Brothers & Lockyer, on 4th June 1948 and is seen at Parliament Street garage in May 1949. One of the Park Royal examples, **AMV 482**, had originally been an Associated Equipment Company Limited demonstrator. It was built in 1932 and was petrol-engined. As Nottingham No. **269** it was placed in service on 5th June 1948 and lasted, as did No. 265, until 1954. It was photographed *(below)* in July 1949. An AEC oil engine had been fitted, resulting in the extended bonnet.

*Postwar trolleybuses*

In 1948 Nottingham's first true postwar trolleybuses were delivered. The batch of 17 comprised four Karrier Ws and 13 BUT 9611Ts. BUT was British United Traction, a joining of forces for trolleybus production of AEC and Leyland. Bodywork seating 56 on all 17 was by Roe. The first of them, Karrier W No. **479** (**KTV 479**), is seen *(above)* when brand new at Wells Road terminus. In a perfectly composed Old Market Square scene *(below)* one of the BUTs, No. **490** (**KTV 490**), was in service in late 1948 alongside motorbuses Nos **56** (**ETV 789**), a 1938 Metro-Cammell-bodied AEC Regent and **776**, formerly 276 and originally 76 (**DAU 455**), which was a 1937 Cravens-bodied AEC Regal. Foglamps positioned as on No. 56, without supporting headlamps, became illegal on 1st January 1949.

*Postwar motorbuses*

*Above:* Although to non-utility specification, the Metro-Cammell bodies on Nottingham's first true postwar motorbuses in 1949 looked much the same as the design introduced by that coachbuilder in 1934. There were 30 AEC Regent IIIs so bodied, the first of which was No. **97** (**KTV 97**), seen here in Wollaton Street in June 1949.

*Below:* In 1948/9 31 Daimler CVD6 chassis were bought. The first ten, Nos 270-9 fitted with Brush bodies, arrived in July 1948. Number **273** (**KTV 273**) is shown at Trent Boulevard in the following month. The Brush bodies were of composite wood and metal construction.

### Brush-bodied Daimlers

*Above:* In September 1948 six British buses, all Daimler double-deckers, were sent to Copenhagen to take part in a trade exhibition. One of the six was Nottingham's No. **278** (**KTV 278**), a Brush-bodied example delivered at the end of July 1948. This detailed view shows its "GB" plate as well as the neat combination stop and direction-indicator lights and the protective corner bumper bars. It was at Calverton Road, Arnold, in July 1950.

*Below:* At the same location a year earlier was another Brush-bodied Daimler, No. **297** (**KTV 297**). This bus had been new in March 1949 and was withdrawn in 1958. The notice in the back window related to an increase in fares.

*Roberts-bodied Daimlers*

*Above:* In addition to the Brush-bodied examples, 15 Daimler CVD6 double-deckers, fleet numbers 280-94, with Roberts all-metal bodies were taken into stock between December 1948 and June 1949. Pristine in its newness and its appearance not compromised by advertising material, No. **287** (**KTV 287**) is seen at Calverton Road, Arnold, in May 1949, when about six weeks old.

*Below:* In February 1956, when they were about seven years old, Roberts-bodied Daimler CVD6s **293/4** (**KTV 293/4**) were standing in Sherwood depot, which provided buses for the Arnold and the main Mapperley services. These 1949 Roberts-bodied Daimlers were withdrawn from Nottingham service between 1959 and 1963.

*The first 8ft-wide motorbuses*

Following the Roberts-bodied Daimlers *(see page 33)*, 41 AEC Regent IIIs arrived from the same coachbuilder between November 1949 and March 1950. They were noteworthy as having been built to the then new maximum width of eight feet - the first such motorbuses for Nottingham. With fleet numbers 301-41, they incorporated an interesting example of dual-sourcing for their air-braking equipment, Nos 301-18 having units by Westinghouse and 319-41 by Clayton-Dewandre. In the upper picture No. **314** (**KTV 314**) was caught in Trinity Square on service 17 to Bulwell; No. **332** (**KTV 332**) *(below)*, also on the 17, was in Hucknall Road. Both are 1950 photographs. These buses served the city well until the last was withdrawn in 1966.

## *The postwar standard trolleybus*

From the end of 1949 delivery began of a batch of no fewer than 102 BUT 9641T three-axled trolleybuses intended to replace the remaining pre-1940 vehicles. They were numbered 500-601 and the first 25 (500-24) were to the newly permitted 8ft width; they arrived in the fleet between November 1949 and May 1950 and the remainder (525-601), which were 7ft 6ins wide, came between August 1950 and June 1952. All had bodywork seating 70 constructed by Brush Coachworks, of Loughborough, though the later ones were completed by Willowbrook when Brush ceased production of bus bodywork. The 8ft-wide vehicles were for the Carlton - Wollaton Park service, the only one in need of large vehicles to be authorised for eight-footers. All routes were later authorised but bodywork for the 7ft 6ins vehicles had already been constructed. Electric motors for these vehicles were triple-sourced, some coming from each of English Electric, Crompton Parkinson and Metro-Vick. Two of the 8ft-wide examples are illustrated: No. **501** (**KTV 501**) in Parliament Street *(above)* in July 1952 and *(below)* No. **506** (**KTV 506**) at the bottom of King Street in September 1953.

*Postwar trolleybuses*

*Above:* The classic view of a postwar British trolleybus - clean, unfussy, pollutionless, effortlessly powered traction in a wide suburban dual-carriageway. Nottingham's 8ft-wide BUT 9641T No. **508** (**KTV 508**) was at Wollaton Park, Middleton Boulevard, in August 1950.

*Below:* This scene at Nottingham Road, Basford, dates from April 1966 and includes three trolleybuses. The two identifiable ones are Nos **507/16** (**KTV 507/16**). There is again very little other traffic in a wide city thoroughfare and this seems the ideal way to move into and out of the city centre. It is really very hard to understand the British panic rush to scrap serviceable, efficient electric traction, particularly when it is recalled how many such systems have been nurtured and invested in and still silently and efficiently serve towns and cities in other parts of Europe and the world, thus reducing the pollution count in no small way.

***Trolleybuses in the Nottingham landscape***

***Above:*** The difference in width between the 7ft 6ins and 8ft versions of the Brush bodied BUT 9641T three-axled trolleybus is well shown in this December 1953 Trent Bridge view of No. **576** (**KTV 576**) on the left with, alongside, eight-footer No. **506** (**KTV 506**).

***Below:*** Highbury Road, Bulwell, in August 1964. Number **550** (**KTV 550**), a 7ft 6ins-wide machine, on the way from Bulwell Hall to Colwick Road passes the road leading to Bulwell depot. The view includes the complicated overhead wiring layout into and out of the side road in both directions.

*Opposite page:* The Old Market Square was on the through trolleybus service 43 from Bulwell to Trent Bridge. BUT No. **546 (KTV 546)** is seen approaching the loading stand for Trent Bridge in August 1965.

*This page:* On the same service, arrival at Trent Bridge for No. **585 (KTV 585)** in March 1953 is made difficult by two parked motorcycles and a fine prewar Austin 7 "Ruby".

**Trolleybuses in the Nottingham landscape**

*Above:* St Peter's Square at the foot of Wheeler Gate in August 1951 with new BUT 9641T trolleybus No. **562** (**KTV 562**) *en route* to Trent Bridge on service 43. The AEC motorbus in the background was one of those acquired from Halifax in the late 1940s *(see pages 28/9)*.

*Below:* An interesting comparison at Trent Bridge in November 1951 juxtaposes one of the new six-wheeled BUT 9641Ts with Brush bodywork, No. **527** (**KTV 527**), and No. **438** (**AFU 153**), a 1938 Park Royal-bodied AEC four wheeler, which came second-hand to Nottingham from Cleethorpes *(see page 18)*.

### Unusual trolleybus activity

*Above:* Glasgow Corporation **TBS2** (**FYS 766**), a BUT "standee" trolleybus bodied by East Lancashire Coachbuilders, was briefly on hire as a demonstrator to Nottingham in January/February 1953. Geoffrey Atkins tracked it down one February evening at Nottingham Road terminus.

*Below:* Here is another view from that unique occasion on 1st July 1966 when 8ft-wide BUT No. **506** (**KTV 506**) ran a commemorative last journey the day after the normal trolleybus service had ceased operation. Number 506 was attracting some attention at the King Street/Queen Street terminal point.

*Special-purpose vehicles*

***Above:*** One of the 1939 AEC Regents with Metro-Cammell bodywork, No. 31 (**FTO 614**), was seriously damaged in an accident in April 1950 and was prematurely withdrawn - the rest of the batch of 16 were withdrawn between 1955 and 1958. FTO 614 was rebuilt as a tower wagon with the fleet number **802**, and still exists in preservation at Sandtoft Transport Centre.

***Below:*** Number **507** (**GTV 404**) was a 1943 Ford 10-cwt van, which ran until 1956 in Nottingham service as an inspector's van. In this October 1949 view taken inside Trent Bridge works it had been fitted with a loudspeaker for public address duties.

*New single-deckers and second-hand low-height double-deckers*

*Above:* The single-deck fleet was augmented in June/July 1951 when four East Lancashire-bodied AEC Regal IIIs were delivered. At that time only three single-deckers were required, for use under low bridges. These 35-seat, rear-entrance buses were numbered 700-3. Number **700** (**LTV 700**) is seen when brand new in Stanhope Street, outside Parliament Street garage. It was withdrawn in 1962, seven years earlier than the other three of the batch.

*Below:* Nottingham's Clifton Estate service needed low-height buses and in 1952 seven Daimler CWA6s with Duple 53-seat lowbridge bodies were bought from Bradford Corporation. Extensively refurbished before entering service between October 1952 and February 1954, they were withdrawn in 1958. Nottingham No. **47** (**DKY 496**) had been Bradford No. 496.

*<< Opposite page:* Park Royal-bodied AEC Regal III No. **142** (**OTV 142**) was first licensed on 1st December 1953; the vehicle behind it, No. **174** (**BTO 18**), was withdrawn on 31st of the same month, which neatly dates the picture for us. The location was Long Row, with the city's Council House in the background.

*This page:* Nottingham's last AEC Regent IIIs were delivered in 1954. There were 51 of them, all with Park Royal bodies. For the last ten, Nos 199-208, the order was changed to one for alloy-framed lowbridge bodies seating 53, for use on the Clifton Estate service. In the picture above, the first of the ten, No. **199** (**SAU 199**), was at Broad Marsh in October 1954 when six months old. The lower picture shows the reason for the lowbridge buses. In March 1958, No. 199 had just passed beneath the Great Central Railway bridge in Wilford Lane.

**The AEC Regent Mark V**

*Above:* Sixty-five AEC Regent Mark Vs with Park Royal bodywork were ordered for 1955/6 delivery. They were the last AEC Regents bought new by Nottingham. Number **238** (**UTV 238**), new in March 1956, was photographed in Milton Street in September of that year. These buses were the first purchased new since 1939 to have separate service number apertures. The indicator layout was similar to an earlier Manchester/Salford design, whence (from Salford City Transport) had come NCT's recent new Chief Engineer, Frank Thorp.

*Below:* The eventual change to rear-engined buses brought with it a livery change, which was retrospectively applied to older buses in the fleet, as shown by AEC Regent V No. **245** (**XTO 245**), which had been new in September 1956. It was at Trent Boulevard, West Bridgford, in February 1971. A glance at the picture above will confirm the opinion of many observers that the new livery was no improvement.

## Nottingham buys the Leyland Titan

The AEC Regent Vs of 1955/6 had synchromesh gearboxes. This specification allowed Leyland Motors Limited to tender for Nottingham's requirements and in 1958/9, under General Manager Ben England, 44 Titan PD2/40s were taken into stock. There would be no more Titans, although they were not quite the last traditional-style buses in the fleet. The bodies were by Metro-Cammell and were a modified four-bay version of the rather ungainly "Orion" style. Numbers 2 - 33 had steel-framed Mark V bodies and 34 - 45 the alloy-framed Mark IV version. Number **16** (**16 ATO**) *(above)* was one of the 1958 arrivals. It is seen passing through Parliament Street garage's bus washer in May 1964. In the picture below No. **28** (**28 ATO**), sporting an experimental livery, was in Trinity Square in May 1962.

**Demonstrators**

*Above:* The use of demonstrators was a perennial feature of bus operation in Nottingham. This one was the experimental AEC Regent Mark IV, a type that did not go into production. It had an underfloor engine and a 60-seat body by Crossley. It was running on AEC's Middlesex County Council trade plates **368 H,** and would thus not have carried passengers in service. This picture was taken in September 1949 at AEC's Brook Street, Nottingham, depot, where it was shown to all interested operators in the area.

*Below:* The Daimler Freeline was introduced in 1951 as an underfloor-engined "standee" bus for 60 passengers, with 30 seated. Duple-bodied **LRW 377** was the second one built, and was demonstrated to Nottingham in January/February 1953.

## Demonstrators

*Above:* In January 1954 an experimental lightweight AEC Regent with 7.7-litre engine and synchromesh gearbox, a specification that paved the way for the Regent Mark V, was demonstrated to Nottingham City Transport. Middlesex-registered **7194 H** was painted in the elaborate livery of City of Oxford Motor Services.

*Below:* The Daimler CD650, with 10.6-litre engine, was a direct challenge to the 9.6-litre AEC Regent and the 9.8-litre Leyland PD2. It was not successful despite being demonstrated to many operators, some of whom, like Nottingham, were already Daimler users. On Coventry trade plates **020 WK**, the Roe-bodied CD650 demonstrator, which was registered KHP 998, is seen inside Parliament Street garage in September 1954. It later passed to the independent operator Beckett, of Bucknall.

## Concealed radiator demonstrators

*Above:* AEC Regent V **159 JHX**, registered, as usual for an AEC demonstrator, by Middlesex County Council, was built in June 1956 and finished in a version of Birmingham Corporation's livery. The Park Royal 65-seat body also had a Birmingham-style front destination display. Mechanically it was aimed at operators of preselector-gearbox buses, being fitted with two-pedal Monocontrol epicyclic transmission. It is seen in Huntingdon Street, Nottingham, in September 1956.

*Below:* Daimler's Coventry-registered **VKV 99**, a CVG6-30 model (and thus Gardner-engined) with Willowbrook bodywork, was in Nottingham's Trinity Square in December 1958.

### New Generation Demonstrators

The rear-engined revolution, or - rather - the revolution that allowed operators to lobby for and eventually gain the introduction of driver-only working, thus alleviating recruitment problems and saving some of the cost of employing conductors, was unstoppable. Thus, even with a vehicle that was initially unreliable - decidedly troublesome, indeed - Leyland, and later Daimler and Bristol with less challenging vehicles, were assured of a good market for their new designs. The PDR1/1 Atlantean demonstrator **398 JTB** *(above)* was at Broad Marsh in June 1960. Guy Motors had less luck with their Wulfrunian. It had more or less the same configuration of driver-controlled passenger entry and exit, but the engine was between him and the boarding platform. The idea was a good one, but major design faults led to operator dissatisfaction with the few that were sold. Demonstrator **7800 DA** was in Trinity Square *(below)* in May 1961.

**Daimler and AEC still in the Fight**

*Above:* The first Daimler Fleetline chassis built had a Weymann body. Outwardly similar to contemporary Atlanteans, it was in fact a superior design both operationally and mechanically. **7000 HP** was sent to Birmingham in January 1961 and had a version of that operator's livery. The following June it was at Broad Marsh, Nottingham. Both this and the Atlantean led to substantial orders from Nottingham.

*Below:* AEC, having no rear-engined design in its portfolio, was still trying hard with the traditionally laid-out double-decker, by March 1963 in the form of the low-height Renown. **7552 MX**'s visit to Nottingham resulted in one order, for 42 buses delivered in 1965, but the battle was lost: AEC Renowns needed conductors; the rear-engined designs won the day.

## 1970s Demonstrators

*Above:* Before leaving, for the moment, Geoffrey Atkins's comprehensive coverage of vehicles on demonstration in Nottingham, we shall look ahead a few years to 1972 and 1973. In the former year the Metro-Scania single-decker **VWD 451H** was tried in Nottingham. In these days of blanket coverage by foreign chassis, it is hard to recall how strange this vehicle was over three decades ago.

*Below:* For as long as motor vehicles have existed attempts to find an efficient self-contained electric vehicle have been made and have failed - at least for passenger transport use; the less demanding rôles of milk and railway parcels delivery, for example, have seen some modest though impermanent success. In August 1973 Nottingham tried a Crompton battery-electric bus, **CWO 516K**, on the City Centre free service 88. The Willowbrook-bodied machine would run only 40 miles on a charge and the second half of its duty had to be performed by a diesel-engined vehicle.

### Daimler Fleetlines

*Above:* Nineteen-sixty-two saw the first Daimler Fleetlines in the Nottingham fleet. A batch of 18, fitted with Park Royal 77-seat bodies, entered service in November and December. In the latter month brand new No. **51** (**51 NAU**) was photographed at Broad Marsh.

*Below:* The 1962 Fleetlines were followed in 1963 by a further batch of 31, this time with Northern Counties bodywork. These were also 77-seaters and the design allowed interchangeability of certain parts with the Park Royal version. Number **72** (**72 RTO**) was in Milton Street, outside Victoria station, in June 1963. Note the different proportions of green and cream in the liveries of Nos 51 and 72, the latter being the new standard.

### Rebodied Daimler Fleetlines

Four of the 1963 Fleetlines were, in 1975/6, rebodied by the original coachbuilder, Northern Counties, when they were found to be in need of substantial body repairs. Numbers 75, 77, 82 and 83 were the chosen quartet and the exercise was thought worthwhile to counteract the difficulties being caused by delays in deliveries of new chassis. Northern Counties scrapped the original bodies after salvaging some parts for use in the new units. The "Nottingham look" was well-established by the time of these rebodyings and the straight rear profile was an interesting feature. Number **77** (**77 RTO**) was at Parliament Street garage in September 1977 *(above)* and No. **75** (**75 RTO**) was outside Trent Bridge works in July 1978.

## Leyland Atlanteans and AEC Renowns

*Above:* The first batch of Leyland Atlanteans arrived in 1964: a cautious order for ten of the revised and, it was hoped, improved PDR1/2 version. Numbers 401-10 had Northern Counties 77-seat bodies and No. **406** (**BTV 406B**) is seen in another Milton Street shot close to Victoria railway station. These buses, the first of which was exhibited at the 1964 Commercial Motor Show, introduced the distinctive "Nottingham Look" that was to become so familiar on many hundreds of the city's buses.

*Below:* In 1965, 42 AEC Renown 70-seaters with Weymann (35) or Northern Counties 70-seat bodies arrived as part of the trolleybus replacement fleet. Number **391** (**FAU 391C**), one of the seven Northern Counties examples, was photographed in November 1966 at the Mapperley terminus of service 9, which was not a former trolleybus service.

### *The 1966 Daimler Fleetlines*

In 1966, after the purchase in 1964/5 of 84 PDR1/2 Leyland Atlanteans, Nottingham returned to Daimler with an order for 30 Fleetlines. Numbers 95-124 were bodied by Metro-Cammell as 76-seaters. They had shallower upper-deck saloons with a headroom of 5ft 10½ins and the front of the upper saloon was redesigned. In the upper picture, taken in September 1966, No. **104** (**HTO 104D**), in original condition, is shown inbound on Mansfield Road on service 49 Bestwood Park Estate to Trinity Square. The entire batch was converted to 72-seat dual-doorway specification by Seddon in 1970/1 for driver-only operation, exemplified by No. **109** (**HTO 109D**) at the foot of King Street *(below)* in August 1972. This bus was extensively damaged by fire in January 1973 and dismantled by the operator.

### *The 1967 Leyland Atlanteans*

Similar Metro-Cammell 76-seat bodies were specified for a batch of 15 PDR1/2 Atlanteans in 1967. The fleet numbers were 485-99. In 1969/70 eight of them were converted as 72-seat dual-doorway buses for driver-only operation. The work was done in Nottingham City Transport's own workshops. The other seven were never rebuilt with a second doorway but were nevertheless adapted for operation without a conductor. Number **486** (**JTV 486E**) was photographed *(above)* in original condition at Broad Marsh in February 1967. This was one of the seven not rebuilt. Number **487** (**JTV 487E**) was the lowest-numbered of the eight rebuilt examples. It was converted in January 1969 and is seen *(below)* at Trent Bridge in the following June.

### Fleetlines and Swifts

*Above:* In 1967/8 a further 35 Northern Counties-bodied Daimler Fleetlines, similar to Nos 95-124, were allocated fleet numbers 125-59. All were converted to two-door specification in 1969/70. Number **152** (**MTO 152F**) in original condition was at Broad Marsh in April 1968 with two Barton Leyland PD1 Titans in the background.

*Below:* Nottingham, never a big user of single-deck buses after the 1930s, bought six rear-engined AEC Swifts, Nos 707-12, in 1969. The dual-doorway 43-seat bodies were by Northern Counties. Many parts of the body were interchangeable with those on contemporary double-deckers. The first of them, No. **707** (**PTO 707G**), was at Trent Boulevard in February 1971. The Swift was not one of AEC's better models and Nottingham's six were withdrawn and sold in 1975 after an exceptionally short life by the standards of the time. They were bought by Grimsby-Cleethorpes Transport who managed a further five or six years from them. These AEC Swifts were among the first buses in the Nottingham fleet to qualify for the New Bus Grant *(see page 61)*.

***The Acquisition of the West Bridgford Fleet***

*Above:* The 28-bus fleet of neighbouring West Bridgford Urban District Council was taken over by Nottingham City Transport on the night of 28th/29th September 1968. West Bridgford's fleet numbers 31-3 were Reading-bodied 59-seat lowbridge AEC Regent Vs dating from 1957/8. Number 31 (**XVO 329**) became Nottingham's No. **200**, as seen at Broad Marsh in March 1969.

*Below:* West Bridgford had bought two AEC Renowns, Nos 41/2, in 1965. They had East Lancashire 75-seat bodies and became Nottingham's 393/4. Number **393** (**BRR 241C**) was photographed in December 1968, also at Broad Marsh.

## The Bus Grant

Nineteen-sixty-eight was the year of the introduction of the New Bus Grant facility, whereby if buses were purchased with certain features which fitted them for driver-only operation, 25% of the cost, later increased to 50%, would be refunded by the Department of Transport. The first Nottingham double-deckers to qualify were Leyland PDR1A/1 Atlanteans Nos 501-22 in 1968/9. They had Northern Counties 76-seat dual-doorway bodies. Number **502** (**PTO 502G**) was four months old in a June 1969 view taken near Wilford Bridge *(above)*. Number **503** (**PTO 503G**), seen *(below)* in Long Row in March 1976, was withdrawn in June of that year after suffering fire damage and was later dismantled.

### The Standard for the 1970s

*Above:* Atlanteans 501-22 had been of an interim design; 1970's PDR1A/1 Atlanteans 523-39 really set the Nottingham standard for the next decade or so. Their Northern Counties 77-seat high-floor bodies reverted to the 3ft 11ins pillar pitch used on all Fleetlines and Atlanteans up to Nos 159 and 499. Number **539** (**STO 539H**) was in the demonstration park at the 1970 Earls Court Commercial Motor Show.

*Below:* Hot on the heels of Nos 523-39 came six 75-seat low-height versions of the same design on Atlantean PDR1/3 chassis, numbered 395-400. Number **400** (**VAU 400J**) was on display when brand new in January 1971 in the Old Market Square. These buses were purchased for the Clifton Estate service.

### Open Tops and 80-Seaters

*Above:* Numbers 160-84, Willowbrook-bodied 77-seat Fleetlines, were delivered in 1973. One of them, No. **161** (**ETO 161L**), was rebuilt as an open-top sightseeing bus in the mid-eighties. It was later sold to the Guide Friday operation at Stratford upon Avon. In this September 1984 view it was leaving Victoria bus station on a Sunday working to Newstead Abbey.

*Below:* New in October 1980, No. **692** (**MNU 692W**) was an Atlantean AN68 with Northern Counties 80-seat bodywork. It was in Mansfield Road in March 1981.

### The Last Atlanteans and the Search for a Successor

*Above:* The New Bus Grant was reduced from 50% to 40% on 31st March 1981. Northern Counties were able to complete only 15 of an order for 25 Atlanteans before that date, and there was a scramble to hurry the remaining ten chassis across to Charles H Roe, of Leeds, for bodying in time to avoid losing the Grant money. Roe-bodied No. 476 (**NNN 476W**) was leaving Victoria bus station when brand new in March 1981.

*Below:* In 1982, with the AN68 Atlantean going out of production, alternatives were sought. Two Dennis Falcons with Mercedes V6 engines and East Lancashire dual-doorway 88-seat bodies were ordered, Nos 396/7, of which No. **397** (**XRA 397Y**) is seen turning out of High Street into Victoria Street in June 1984.

### Citybuses and Lions

*Above:* Two Volvo underfloor-engined B10MD Citybuses were also tried. They arrived in November 1983, were numbered 398/9, and had 86-seat dual-doorway bodies built at Blackburn by East Lancashire Coachbuilders. The first, No. **398** (**A398 CRA**), was in Victoria Street in June 1984 bound for Sneinton Dale.

*Below:* The underfloor-engined theme continued in 1986 with Nos 392-4, Leyland-DAB Lions with Northern Counties bodies. Number **393** (**D393 TAU**), new in October 1986, is seen in February 1995 in King Street, with Alexander-bodied Volvo B6 No. **512** (**M512 TRA**) and Leyland National Mark II No. **19** (**ETT 319Y**), which had been new to the Devon Area Health Authority in 1983, but had come to Nottingham from Athelstan, of Malmesbury, in September 1989.

### Scanias and Olympians

*Above:* In 1989-92 no fewer than 28 Scania N112DR and N113DRB double-deckers entered the Nottingham fleet. Nineteen were new, two were ex-demonstrators and seven were second-hand. Twenty-seven had Alexander bodies. This is No. **361** (**E200 WHS**), one of the second-hand ones and the odd one out, which was bodied by East Lancashire. It was in King Street in March 1992.

*Below:* Two Leyland Olympians were among the chassis evaluated for possible future use. Numbered 698/9, they were delivered in February 1984. Number **699** (**A699 EAU**) was in more or less the same spot in King Street in June 1984. The 80-seat body was by Northern Counties.

## Atlanteans and Scanias

*Above:* It was rather ironic that, having finally made a reliable vehicle of the Atlantean, Leyland phased it out and that, while all these replacement options were being examined, the final version of the Atlantean, the AN68, had settled down and was efficiently going about its business in many cities, including Nottingham. This one, No. **401** (**JRC 401V**), a 1980 arrival and one of many Nottingham AN68s bodied by East Lancashire Coachbuilders, featured bonded windows on the upper deck. It was photographed at Valley Road, West Bridgford.

*Below:* Number **381** (**E381 ERB**) was a Scania demonstrator licensed in June 1988. The 83-seat body was by Alexander and featured dot-matrix destination displays. This photograph was taken in Trinity Square in February 1989.

**Volvos and a Titan**

*Above:* In addition to the Scania double-deckers in 1988/9, there were six Volvo Citybuses, numbered 330-5. Number **335** (**G335 PAL**) had an Alexander 82-seat body and is seen at Broad Marsh in August 1991. Note the route number screen, not in use, on the nearside above the first window.

*Below:* A famous name was revived with the integrally constructed rear-engined Leyland Titan. London Transport bought a lot, but few were otherwise sold. A demonstrator registered **VAO 488Y** was tried in Nottingham in 1983. In this picture it was at Mapperley Plains heading for Gedling on service 50.

*More Volvos and the Return of Dennis*

*Above:* Nottingham's Nos 485-9, five 1993 Volvo Olympians, were among the last buses to be bodied at the Whalley New Road, Blackburn, premises of East Lancashire coachbuilders (No. 487 was the very last). The final member of the batch, No. **489 (L489 NTO)**, was in Long Row in May 1994.

*Below:* After some decades of absence, Dennis buses returned to Nottingham in the nineteen-nineties. Four Arrows with Northern Counties Paladin 2 bodywork, which had been built in October 1995, were put into service in April 1996. Number **401 (N401 ARA)** is seen in a special livery for the Forest Park & Ride service 303. It was in King Street in April 1996.

### Centenary Celebrations

*Above:* In connection with Nottingham Council's ownership of the city's transport undertaking for 100 years, a milestone reached in 1997, East Lancashire-bodied Scania No. **352** (**L352 MRR**) was painted in the old electric tram livery, with detailed artwork on the rear to represent tram No. 100 and, no doubt, frighten following drivers. It was in Long Row in October 1977.

### Scania Demonstrator

*Below:* A further *(see page 67)* Alexander-bodied Scania N113RB was hired in 1990 and bought in March 1991. Number **360** (**G879 TVS**) was in Shakespeare Street in May 1993.

### Scanias and Titans

*Above:* One of a pair of earlier Scania double-deckers, type BR112DH No. **395** (**EMJ 560Y**), had an East Lancashire body and was taken into the fleet in June 1984. In this photograph it was outside Trent Bridge works in July 1995.

*Below:* London Transport for most of its postwar history was notorious for the wholesale withdrawal and sale of buses that other operators managed to use for many more years. The London Leyland Titans suffered this fate and, in March 1993, Nottingham took two with Gardner engines and Park Royal bodywork, which took fleet numbers 60/1, for evaluation. Number **61** (**CUL 119V**) was in Trinity Square in June 1993.

*Dennis Tridents*

**Above:** Dennis Tridents with East Lancashire bodies started to enter the Nottingham fleet in early 1999. They were the first low-floor double-deckers (in the modern sense of the term). Number **416** (**T416 BNN**) typifies the type. It was in Long Row in August 1999.

*Single-deck Renaissance*

**Below:** Up to the beginning of the 1970s Nottingham did not perceive a big requirement for single-deckers. From 1973, however, a total of 47 Leyland Nationals was acquired. Number **720** (**C720 MRC**) was a 1985 Mark II example, seen in Long Row in August 1995.

## A Move into Coaching

*Above:* As a tentative step into coach operation, two Bedford YRQs, Nos 601/2, were obtained in 1972. They had Willowbrook Expressway 45-seat bodies. Number **602** (**BTV 602K**) is seen in South Parade in June 1975 working service 14 to Brockley Road.

## Single-deckers

*Below:* An earlier, Mark I, 1051 Leyland National, No. **723** (**FAU 723L**), one of a number purchased for free town centre circular services, is seen here working service 31 to Mapperley. It was photographed in King Street in May 1977.

### Development of the Single-deck Fleet

*Above:* In 1984, to test the demand for midibuses, five Bristol LHSL dual-purpose 27-seaters with Eastern Coach Works bodies were acquired from West Yorkshire PTE. They ran for less than two years but did establish that midibus operation was viable. Number **731** (**MUA 45P**) is seen after dark at Broad Marsh in January 1985.

*Below:* Two Leyland Leopard coaches with Duple Dominant II dual-purpose 53-seat bodies to Bus Grant specification arrived in 1980, numbered 798/9. Far removed from NCT's traditional style of business, No. **799** (**GTO 799V**) is here seen leaving Victoria bus station in July 1982 duplicating National Express route 730 to Birmingham. These Leopards were in a cream, brown and orange livery.

## Development of the Single-deck Fleet

*Above:* A distressing, to some observers, trend in the last two decades or so has been the use of hastily converted delivery van chassis for use as public service vehicles. Usually uncomfortable for passengers and hideous to drive, they nonetheless proliferated because they were cheap and readily available. Typical examples in Nottingham were five 1987/8 Renault 23-seaters with Alexander bodywork, which came second-hand from Northampton in 1991/2. They were used mainly on Park & Ride service 304, and No. **103 (E103 JNH)** is seen so employed at Colwick in April 1993.

*Below:* Twenty-five Leyland Lynx Mark I buses were ordered for delivery between March 1988 and December 1989. They were numbered 725-49. Number **731 (E731 BVO)** was on service 89 to Rise Park in Mansfield Road in May 1988.

### Development of the Single-deck Fleet

*Above:* The "upgraded delivery van" syndrome has gradually given way to properly designed and constructed smaller buses, exemplified by the Optare MetroRider 30-seater. Nottingham took 33 between May 1994 and October 1997. Number **206** (**L206 ONU**) of the first batch was photographed in Parliament Street in April 1995.

*Below:* A somewhat larger machine, the low-floor Optare Excel, entered Nottingham service with a batch of five between September 1996 and March 1997. Number **544** (**P544 GAU**), on service 58A to Arnold, is shown in Long Row in 1997.

### Pre- and postwar traffic scenes

Taken from almost the same spot in 1933 and April 1991, 1920 electric tramcar No. **180**, 1931 AEC Regent No. **116** (**TV 4949**), a 1931 Ransomes trolleybus and a Notts & Derby AEC trolleybus are contrasted with Alexander-bodied Scania No. **369** (**G369 RTO**), Leyland National No. **720** (**C720 MRC**), and a pair of midibuses. Number 369 was in a special livery for Park & Ride service 303. Although 1991 is by no means the latest date on a Geoffrey Atkins Nottingham photograph *(see page 79)*, nor is 1933 the earliest, this pair of scenes spanning nearly 60 years epitomises Geoffrey's painstaking recording of the public transport scene in his home city.

### More on that "Nottingham Look"

*Above:* Nottingham's has always been one of the most instantly recognisable of all the municipal fleets; this was particularly so during the sixties, seventies and eighties when a distinct visual identity was applied to rear-engined buses. The Leyland AN68 Atlantean featured strongly in that presentation and No. **547** (**OTO 547M**) could never be confused with any other operator's vehicle.

*Below:* One of the AN68s, new in 1978, was built to a striking external design with front and rear quite different from those of its contemporaries. Number **666** (**ARC 666T**) - an unfortunate number? Certainly it was more than once referred to as "diabolical", though on the other hand many observers thought it the best version of the "Nottingham Look" - was a testbed for bonded windscreen, single-width front door and revised rear profile.

*How it was ...*

In photographs taken by Geoffrey Atkins in 1929 and 2001 (yes, that's 72 years apart, spread across nine decades) advances in bus styling and design complexity are graphically illustrated. The Vickers-bodied single-deck Maudslay was photographed in August 1929 at Parliament Street depot.

*... and how it is [1]*

On 30th May 2001 Geoffrey photographed another No. **666**, a Dennis Trident registered **Y966 DRC**, in Mansfield Road, a stone's throw from his residence.

*How it was ...*

In pictures from the early thirties and the late nineties, Geoffrey Atkins illustrates the decline and resurrection of the tramcar for city use. In 1936 in Mansfield Road cars **195** and **199** illustrate the final appearance of the first generation of Nottingham trams.

*... and how it is [2]*

Three-quarters of a century later Geoffrey was again able to photograph a tram in Nottingham, albeit merely a mock-up of part of a tram body for the new NET system due to open in November 2003. At the end of this two-volume survey of Geoffrey's work in Nottingham, author and publisher wish him well, as - we are sure - do all readers, and we look forward to seeing pictures of those 2003 trams from his camera.